Janice,
I just want to say
thank you guys for
everything! I've seen
your "hearts", now I can't
wait to see your "home".
Always,
Jenny
10/10/01
P.S. Rick thanks
you too!

Decorating Your Heart & Home

Brenda Gay Shumaker

Artwork by Susan Wheeler

HARVEST HOUSE PUBLISHERS
Eugene, Oregon

Brenda Gay Shumaker,
an interior designer for the past 25 years, is the founder of
Designs for Living Ministries, an organization that uses
interior design as a bridge to reach people with the truth of
God's Word. Brenda and her creative ideas have been featured
on many radio and television broadcasts. She is very much in
demand as a speaker at conferences and seminars.

Susan Wheeler
is the creator of Victoria Rose and her compatriots of
Holly Pond Hill, an exquisitely detailed watercolor world of
gentle creatures. Susan resides in Fredericksburg, Texas,
where she lives with her husband, Mark, their four children,
and their numerous pets and farm animals.

Decorating Your Heart and Home

Text copyright © 2001 by Brenda Gay Shumaker
Published by Harvest House Publishers
Eugene, Oregon 97402

All works of art reproduced in this book are copyrighted by Susan Wheeler and licensed by InterArt Licensing,
Bloomington, IN, and may not be copied or reproduced without permission. For more information regarding
artwork featured in this book, please contact:

> InterArt™ Licensing
> P.O. Box 4699
> Bloomington, IN 47402-4699
> 800-457-4045

Library of Congress Cataloging-in-Publication Data

> Shumaker, Brenda Gay, 1948–
> Decorating your heart and home / Brenda Gay Shumaker; artwork by Susan Wheeler.
> p. cm.
> ISBN 0-7369-0421-2 (hardcover)
> 1. House furnishings. 2. Interior decorations. 3. Christian life. I. Title.

> TX311 .S48 2001
> 242'.643--dc21

> 00-059755

Design and production by Koechel Peterson & Associates, Minneapolis, Minnesota

Unless otherwise indicated, Scripture quotations are from the *Holy Bible*, New Living Translation, Copyright©
1996. Used by permission of Tyndale House Publishers, Inc., Wheaton, Illinois 60189. All rights reserved.

Scriptures marked NIV are from the Holy Bible, New International Version®, Copyright © 1973, 1978, 1984 by
the International Bible Society. Used by permission of Zondervan Publishing House.

Scriptures marked NKJV are from the New King James Version. Copyright © 1982 by Thomas Nelson, Inc.
Used by permission. All rights reserved.

Scriptures marked TLB are taken from *The Living Bible*, Copyright © 1971. Used by permission of Tyndale House
Publishers, Inc., Wheaton, Illinois 60189. All rights reserved.

Printed in Hong Kong
01 02 03 04 05 06 07 08 09 10 / NG / 10 9 8 7 6 5 4 3 2 1

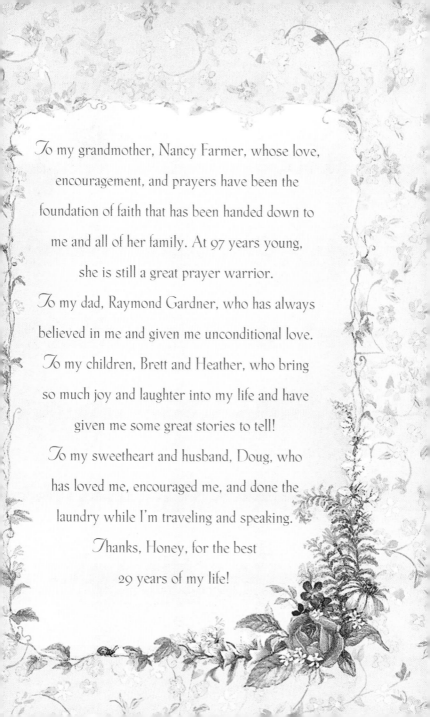

To my grandmother, Nancy Farmer, whose love, encouragement, and prayers have been the foundation of faith that has been handed down to me and all of her family. At 97 years young, she is still a great prayer warrior.

To my dad, Raymond Gardner, who has always believed in me and given me unconditional love.

To my children, Brett and Heather, who bring so much joy and laughter into my life and have given me some great stories to tell!

To my sweetheart and husband, Doug, who has loved me, encouraged me, and done the laundry while I'm traveling and speaking. Thanks, Honey, for the best 29 years of my life!

Acknowledgments

Without the help of many wonderful people I would never have been able to complete this book, or if I did, it wouldn't be in the readable form you have in your hands right now.

My sister, Bobbie Wolgemuth, listened patiently as I called her every morning after I had just written a new devotional, and she always gave me her advice and encouragement.

I also want to thank Carole Bowgren, who took all my devotionals and edited them for punctuation and spelling. The Lord sent you to me at just the right time.

Then there is my friend, assistant, and computer whiz, Jorjia Clinger. She and Dave Syracuse helped me get untangled from the mess I made on the computer (my favorite button is the undo icon). Thanks so much for the hours you spent helping me get this ready to send to the publishers.

Then, last but not least, are the wonderful people at Harvest House Publishers. From the first contact when Ruth Samsel picked up a radio demo tape of my decorating devotionals and told me she thought it would make a good book, to Carolyn McCready working with me when I told her I really wanted Susan Wheeler as the artist for the book— all of you have been so patient with me, and I thank you!

Introduction

Let's take an imaginary walk through the rooms in your home and see if we can make that home of yours even more beautiful and welcoming to those who enter. With this little book, you get ideas not only for decorating the rooms you live in, but also for bringing more joy into the rooms of your heart.

More than twenty-five years ago, as I started out on my first appointment as an interior designer with my shiny, new briefcase in hand and stars in my eyes, I never could have imagined the different roads that God had mapped out for me.

I had my own interior design studio, Heritage House Interiors, for more than 15 years. In 1996 I sold that business and stepped out in faith to travel and speak. One of my speaking topics, "Designs for Joyful Living," was the springboard for my daily radio program of the same name, which airs in the United States and is heard all over the world on the internet. The demo tape of that radio program was picked up by a representative of Harvest House Publishers at a national Christian radio convention. What you are holding in your hand right now is the result of that "chance" meeting.

So prop your feet up and have a cup of tea as you get inspired to decorate your heart and home with some designs for joyful living.

First Impressions

First impressions are really important. When you drive by a house you can tell a lot by how it looks on the outside. Realtors call it "curb appeal." What is the first impression people get when they walk up to your front door? Is the paint peeling? Do the bushes need to be trimmed? Before the door is even opened, visitors can tell a lot about the people living on the inside by what they see on the outside.

Likewise, when people see you for the first time, what impression do they get? Is the paint peeling? Do the bushes need to be trimmed? Is there a light on?

Proverbs 15:30 says, "A cheerful look brings joy to the heart; good news makes for good health." Not only does a cheerful look or smile make us more appealing to others, but it also brings joy to the heart! Maybe sometimes you're having a bad day and not exactly feeling very joyful. Well, according to this verse, there's something you can do. Smile! Have you ever tried to stay grouchy and cranky with a smile on your face? And have you ever noticed that a smile is contagious? When you start smiling at people, they start smiling back. And the second part of this verse says that good news makes for good health. Let's spread that good health around by complimenting or encouraging someone. Be a blessing to someone today, and let God touch that person through you. Your joy will overflow to other people, and the blessings will bounce right back at you. So when someone sees you for the first time, what does that person see? Just as people are drawn to a beautiful house with curb appeal, let them be drawn to you by your cheerful look and glow of joy.

Blueprints

*I*f you've ever built a new house or worked on any type of building project, you know how important blueprints are. I enjoyed designing homes and additions in my interior-design business. I would lay out the floor plan on a piece of graph paper, put the furniture templates in it, and imagine myself walking through each room when it was finished.

Then I would take those floor plans to an architect to draw up the blueprints with the structural supports, wiring, plumbing, and finish elevations. That way, when the house was completed, it would be according to code and wouldn't fall down!

Yes, blueprints are important, and you wouldn't think of starting to build a house without them. Then why do so many people try to build their lives without God's blueprint? We muddle along, making this decision and that choice and going by our feelings, without consulting the Master Architect. In Jeremiah 29:11 we read, " 'For I know the plans I have for you,' says the LORD. 'They are plans for good and not for disaster, to give you a future and a hope.' "

I wonder how many times we ignore God's plan for our lives and end up with a tacky-looking tree house, when He had plans for a beautiful mansion on a hill. Why do we think God is going to make our lives miserable if we give Him full control? No, He has great plans for us. Don't miss out on God's plan for your life by your own disobedience and willfulness. Check His blueprint, the Bible, and you will find that the plan He has for you is filled with joy and prosperity and a hope for the future. So take the scraps of paper you have been using for the plan of your life and have them made into a glorious blueprint by the Master Architect.

Focal Points

It was the first year I was a decorator, and I was sitting in a large group of other designers looking at slides of different room designs. A large, beautiful living room came up on the screen, and the commentator turned to me and asked me to identify the focal point. My heart started pounding, and I could feel a quiver in my hands. Fortunately, I answered correctly when I said, "The fireplace," but there was a scary moment or two when I thought it might be a trick question.

When you're working on the design of a room, you need to find the focal point of that room before you start. It may be the large picture window in a living room, or a fireplace in the family room, or a T.V. in the playroom. The focal point is the center focus of the room, and everything is arranged so that the focal point is the main thing you see when you enter the room. All the furniture is arranged facing the focal point, and your accessories are all positioned to enhance the focus of the room. If you don't have a natural focal point in a room, you can create one. It could be a beautiful bed in the master bedroom or a mural on the wall of a child's room. Whatever it is, a focal point is one thing every room should have.

A focal point is also one thing that every life should have. What is the focal point or focus of your life? What is the central force that all your thoughts revolve around? If someone asked your family or friends what they thought was the most important thing in your life, what would they say?

In Philippians 3:13 Paul says, "No, dear friends, I am still not all I should be, but I am focusing all my energies on this one thing: Forgetting the past and looking forward to what lies ahead, I strain to reach the prize for which God, through Christ Jesus, is calling us up to heaven." Wow! If we would all stay so focused on Christ, we wouldn't be bogged down with things that happened in our past or worried about things that may never happen in the future. Let's remember the words of that great hymn: "Turn your eyes upon Jesus, look full in His wonderful face, and the things of earth will grow strangely dim in the light of His glory and grace."

Log Homes

My husband has always dreamed of someday having a log home. There is a rustic charm and coziness in a log home that never grows old. Since my interior-design business was in Pennsylvania, I had several clients who had log homes.

There are several ways to decorate log homes, but you want to stay with the earthiness and natural feeling of the house. Sometimes log homes are built with the logs exposed on the inside, and if people want the home lighter inside, they put drywall or plaster over the walls. Whatever style was choosen, the main challenge I had was getting enough light around the rooms. Because the logs have a tendency to make things dark, I used curtains or shades on the windows that could be raised up or tied back to let as much light in as possible.

Decorating a log house can be fun as well as a challenge. You can accessorize with old quilts, pitchers with flowers, or antique pictures handed down through the family.

Did you know there's a verse about logs in the Bible? Matthew 7:5 reads, "Hypocrite! First get rid of the log from your own eye; then perhaps you will see well enough to deal with the speck in your friend's eye." So many times we see what's wrong with everybody else, and we don't realize that it's ourselves we need to work on.

I remember for years praying that God would change my husband. When I wasn't nagging or complaining, I was praying, "Please change him, Lord. He's defective!" Well, nothing changed in our marriage, and I was just getting more miserable, so I decided to change my prayer. I said, "Lord, what can I do to make a difference in this marriage?" You see, my attitude changed, and I stopped pointing the finger at my husband and started pointing it at myself. When that happened, God started changing my heart. As I started showing more love and complimenting my husband instead of tearing him down, he started returning that love.

So if you keep finding fault, whether it's in your marriage, in a friendship, or with a family member, just remember this little log story. The only person you can really change is you!

Funny

Have you ever been in someone's home and laughed out loud at something funny they used in their decorating? I have found some really funny things in shops and in my travels that I've brought home and sprinkled around my house in unexpected places. When I hear surprised laughter coming from the guest room, I know someone has moved the sleepy little bear from among the throw pillows on the bed. You see, when someone picks him up, he starts snoring!

On the windowsill over my kitchen sink, I have a little sign that reads, "My three favorite words, LET'S EAT OUT." (My husband just loves that one.) Then in the family room I have a funny frog dressed in a dust cap and apron. On the front of her apron are the words "Housework Makes You Croak." If you walk into the sunroom, on the sill next to my lush, green ivy with the gold tag on the vine that reads "Made in Taiwan" sits a little wooden bunny with a shirt that says "Home of the Dust Bunnies." Now, lest you get the wrong idea that I never cook or clean my house, let me assure you I do...especially when company's coming! Actually, the little plaque that's received the most attention is the one I have in my office which reads, "Behind Every Successful Woman Is a Surprised Man". Well, we won't go into that right now. But I think you get the idea.

Have fun with your decorating. Give yourself and your guests a reason to smile or even chuckle. I read an article that said, on the average, a child laughs out loud 200 times a day—an adult, only four times. Laughter lifts your spirits and gives you a natural face-lift!

Proverbs 17:22 NKJV says, "A merry heart does good, like medicine." Treat yourself to a good laugh today, and you'll feel younger and healthier because of it.

Rattan and Wicker

I was visiting a friend, and we were enjoying lemonade on her airy sunporch. She had decorated her room with rattan furniture, and it looked great. Rattan and wicker furniture have really become popular, and people are using them not only on porches and sunrooms, but also for family rooms, bedrooms, and many other rooms in the house. If you have a room that is small or you don't want a heavy look in it, then wicker or rattan would be ideal. Many times this furniture comes with glass-top tables and is available in various colors or stains.

The fabrics you choose can brighten up a room, and most of the time the cushions are reversible, so you get twice the wear from them.

Rattan and wicker are made from a porous reed-type branch that is soaked in water so it can be bent and shaped to create the furniture pieces. Just as the master craftsman had a design in mind when he bent the branch, so God had a plan in mind when He made us.

In Psalm 139:14-16 it says, "Thank you for making me so wonderfully complex! Your workmanship is marvelous—and how well I know it. You saw me before I was born. Every day of my life was recorded in your book. Every moment was laid out before a single day had passed." Even before you were born, God could see you, and He had a plan for your life.

There are so many forks in the roads of our lives, and unless we get His direction and guidance, we might make a wrong turn or head down a road that is not His will. You might ask, "How do I know what God's will is for my life?" Well, the closer we are to Him, the better we know Him, and He will either close doors or open them.

The next time you come to that fork in the road, spend time in prayer and get into God's Word. If you stay close to Him, He will make clear the design He has planned for your life.

Fireplaces

There's nothing more cozy and inviting than a fireplace. In the winter a roaring fire will make the whole room come alive and just seem to warm you by looking at it.

In the summer, or in the seasons when you're not using the fireplace, a large basket of flowers or scented pinecones can take the place of the blazing logs. I like changing the mantel piece for the seasons, which gives the whole room a new look. A fireplace is not only for the mood or ambience of a room, but also for fun times of making popcorn with a long-handled popcorn cooker or roasting hot dogs on long skewers.

Today our fireplaces are for our enjoyment, but they were a necessary and very functional part of everyday living in days gone by. Not only did people use fireplaces for heating and cooking, but also for making their utensils and shoeing their horses.

In Proverbs 27:21 we read, "Fire tests the purity of silver and gold, but a person is tested by being praised." What happens when you get praised? Do you get all puffed up and try to get more accolades? A person of character and integrity doesn't do things to get praise, but if he is praised, he gives it right back to God. After all, everything we are and everything we're able to do comes from God.

The next time you see a chance to do something good, try doing it without anyone knowing it was you. That way it won't be the applause of men that you'll be rewarded with, but the blessings of God who sees all and knows all.

Remodeling

Have you ever gone past a charming older home that was a bit run-down and imagined how that house would look if it were remodeled? I loved working on remodeling projects because there was such a difference in the before and after.

Sometimes a face-lift will entail just painting and papering, or you might find yourself doing a more involved remodeling with a new kitchen, bathroom, or other major construction. The best idea is to have an experienced builder tell you how much needs to be done in the initial stage so you won't find yourself having to redo floors or supports later on. Yes, the satisfaction of seeing a finished project is so rewarding that you'll find it was worth all the work.

When we accept Christ as our Savior, He does a remodeling job on us. Second Corinthians 5:17 tells us, "What this means is that those who become Christians become new persons. They are not the same anymore, for the old life is gone. A new life has begun!" We are changed from the inside out. We have different desires, different attitudes, and we act differently. Why? Because we have a new Spirit inside us, controlling us.

God's Holy Spirit will change us to become more like Him. But He doesn't come in like an invading force. No, we have to invite Him in and give Him our lives 100 percent. Maybe you've invited Him in the door and left Him standing in the hall. The rest of the house looks as run-down and shabby as it did before. You've held onto old attitudes, anger, unforgiveness, or whatever it is in your life that needs to be cleaned out. Give God the key to your life so He can remodel you 100 percent. You'll find that the more you let Him work in you, the more you will be refreshed with joy and newness of life.

Stained Glass

I remember sitting in church as a child, being mesmerized by the colorful beams of light shining down through the stained-glass windows in our church sanctuary. Some of the most magnificent windows I've seen have been stained glass. Once only found in grand cathedrals or exquisite mansions, stained glass is now used in many ways.

I love putting some stained glass in a foyer so the sunlight can radiate through it and shoot prismatic beams of light all around the entryway. Stained glass is beautiful in lamps, coffee tables, mirrors, or just in sun catchers hanging in a window. In designing rooms that have no access to an exterior wall, I've put stained-glass windows in a wall between two rooms so the light from one room can filter in through the stained glass of the windowless room. It's fun seeing all the different ways you can use stained glass.

But what is a stained-glass creation made of? Broken pieces of glass. Psalm 51:17 says, "The sacrifice you want is a broken spirit. A broken and repentant heart, O God, you will not despise." You see, not until we come to God and lay ourselves broken and repentant before Him, can we become all that He wants us to be. Just as the master artist cannot use the stained glass until it is broken, God will not use us until we are broken and spilled out at His feet. He gently picks up all the pieces, cleans them, polishes them, and assembles them to create a beautiful masterpiece. Then, when His light shines through us, we truly become a thing of beauty.

So are there things in your life that have made you rigid and disobedient to God? Come broken and repentant before Him, and He will take your broken pieces and make a masterpiece out of your life.

Neutrals

*I*n decorating your house, have you ever purchased something in a neutral color just because it was "safe"? I've had clients call me to help with a room, and when I walk in, everything is beige or eggshell. They were afraid to pick colors that may not be right, so they stayed with everything neutral. Well, with the right combination of colors and patterns, your rooms can go from boring to beautiful. Move out of the neutral zone and step into the world of dynamic design.

In Revelation, Jesus was talking about Christians who were in the neutral zone. In chapter 3 and verses 15 and 16, He says, "I know all the things you do, that you are neither hot or cold. I wish you were one or the other! But since you are like lukewarm water, I will spit you out of my mouth!"

For many years I was in that neutral zone. Oh, I was a Christian and had accepted Christ as my Savior. I went to church and prayed before meals—but there was something missing. I was a nominal Christian who was trying to do everything myself and was too busy to spend quality time with God every day. It wasn't until my mother died that I found I needed the comfort of basking in the presence of God. I spent more time with the Lord in prayer. I was hungry for His Word and couldn't wait to find out what special verse He had for me that day. I told my sister, Bobbie, that I felt as if I had lived my Christian life for many years in black and white, and now I've stepped into Technicolor and 3–D!

If you feel as if you have been wandering around in the neutral zone in your Christian life, then step a little closer in your walk with Christ. He will take your hand and lead you into a more exciting, dynamic, and victorious relationship with Him.

Birdbaths

Part of our interior design is what we see outside when we sit in the rooms of our homes. In a real sense, the view from our rooms is part of the design of that room.

I love sitting in my kitchen and looking out the window at the hummingbirds whirling around the feeder, or the cardinals or other birds pecking at the seed. I have a waterfall that attracts all kinds of birds and small animals. The birds come and flutter in the shallow water on the rocks and take a bath, while the squirrels and chipmunks drink from the refreshing, cascading water in the pond. We even had a deer in the backyard! It was such a dry, hot summer that animals which usually stayed in the woods came into our yard for a drink of water. I really enjoy the entertainment of sitting in my kitchen and looking at the cast of players that come into our backyard.

When I saw the deer, it reminded me of Psalm 42:1 where it says, "As the deer pants for streams of water, so I long for you, O God." What are you thirsting for? So many times we thirst for the things of this world, and then when we finally get them, we realize they don't really satisfy like we thought they would. Whether it's something new you just can't live without, or that promotion at work, or the desire to be married, stop, and ask yourself, "Is there anything I desire more than God?" Just as that deer was so thirsty for water, let us be thirsty for the living water that can only be found in a close, intimate relationship with God.

The more you stay focused on Him and long for special time with Him, the more He will fill you with His love and joy!

Traffic

*H*ave you ever noticed when you're at a party or gathering at someone's house that the guests travel in a certain traffic pattern? When you're decorating your home, you should keep in mind the traffic patterns, or in other words, the way people walk through your rooms. The traffic pattern is determined by the way we arrange the furniture and the placement of the doors and entryways in the rooms. The furniture should be arranged so that people can walk through and into the adjoining rooms without tripping over furniture that is placed too close together or blocking easy access to doorways.

When we built our house, I wanted French doors between the living room and family room. Instead of putting those doors on hinges, I had them made as pocket doors so they would slide into the wall when we didn't want them closed, and they were out of the way. This provides a more open flow pattern when we have a large group over.

Also, I have a large island in the center of my kitchen that is great as a serving table or buffet when we have dinner parties or lots of family for Thanksgiving or Christmas. It keeps things moving, and there are no dead ends as the guests follow the path into other rooms.

Just as a good traffic pattern in your home keeps your guests from becoming tangled and confused, God has created a traffic pattern for the path on which we should walk. In Psalm 16:11 (NKJV) David prays, "You will show me the path of life; in Your presence is the fullness of joy."

When we start going our own way and get off God's path that He has marked out for us, we start bumping into difficulties and getting bogged down with problems. Stay on God's path of life, and you will always be walking in His presence and have fullness of joy.

Baskets

A tisket, a tasket, a green-and-yellow basket.... Remember "ring-around-the-rosy"? It's been a long time since I played that game with my children, and even though the ring-around-the-rosy is gone, the baskets are still alive and well at my house. Just ask my husband, and he will tell you I have a thing about baskets. But I can't help it—they are great for so many things.

I have a basket in the family room to hold magazines and newspapers. There's one on the hearth with scented pinecones. There's a big old basket on the counter in the kitchen that I use to hold bread, bagels, and muffins. I put one in the guest room with little toiletries that might come in handy, and in the bathroom I have potpourri in a basket.

Baskets can be round, square, oval, in the shape of ducks, and even a half basket hanging on the front door with flowers in it. But I have to say my favorite basket in the house is God's basket. God's basket is a little oval basket in my

sunroom, where I sit to have my quiet time with Him. If I have a problem or find myself worrying about something, I write it on a piece of paper and put it in God's basket.

In Philippians 4:6, we are told, "Don't worry about anything; instead, pray about everything. Tell God what you need, and thank him for all he has done." You see, when we are worrying, we are not really trusting.

I think of it as having a tape player in our heads. When we find that nagging, worrisome, negative tape playing in our minds, we should take it out and replace it with a praise-and-thanksgiving tape. That's the only thing that will turn our thoughts and minds to God and all the blessings He has showered on us. So the next time you find yourself faced with a problem or a worry, just write it on a piece of paper and put it in God's basket. Pray about it, and then thank and praise Him for His faithfulness as He replaces that worry with His peace and joy.

Engraved Things

From sports trophies to silver or brass accessories, engraved items can add a charm and individuality to almost any room. If you go into gift shops or down to the mall, you see all kinds of gifts that can be engraved or personalized.

I had a frame engraved with the engagement party date of a future bride and groom. Then I took a picture of the couple at the party and framed it in the special engraved frame that will always be a memory for them. When my husband's parents celebrated their twenty-fifth wedding anniversary, they were given a beautiful engraved silver tea service with the date of their wedding and the date of that very special anniversary. We inherited that tea service, and every time I serve from it, I enjoy seeing their wedding date engraved there. When we built our house, I had the glass above our front door engraved with a Bible verse. It's a great reminder for us every time we look at it, and it's a testimony to all those who come to our front door.

Did you know that the Bible talks about something that is engraved? In Isaiah 49:15,16 (NIV) the Lord says, "I will not forget you! See, I have engraved you on the palms of my hands." God loves us so much He will never forget us. We are indelibly imprinted on His hands. How could He ever forget us when the scars on His hands will always remind Him of the price He paid for us?

Many times we get so busy with day-to-day life that we forget to set aside some time to spend with the Lord. Even though we sometimes forget Him, He never forgets us. So the next time you see something engraved, just remember the outstretched hands of the Savior, with your name engraved in the scars. Reach out to Him today; He's patiently waiting to spend time with you.

Old Frames

*H*ave you ever wandered around in antique shops or flea markets and seen something old and thought how beautiful it would be if it were restored? One of my dad's favorite hobbies was restoring old frames. He would pick up old frames with pieces missing and restore them so they looked like new. Since Dad is a dentist, he would take an impression of the good side and create a new piece to fit into the side that was missing—the same way he took impressions of people's teeth. Then he would fit that new piece into the frame, and after it was painted gold or silver, it looked brand-new.

Mom had portraits done of my sisters and me when we turned 16, and Daddy restored a beautiful gilded frame for each of us. When I got married, Dad gave me a beautiful floor-to-ceiling pier mirror that I still have in my living room today. It's one of my favorite things because of the labor of love Dad took in making it.

It's hard to believe anything beautiful could be made from some of the dirty, cracked, and broken frames Dad brought home, but he could see the potential in them. I'm sure we probably look that way to God sometimes, but He can see the potential in us. In James 1:4 (NIV) it says, "Perseverance must finish its work so that you may be mature and complete, not lacking anything." God wants to work on us to fill in the parts that are missing.

He's taking an impression of Christ and making a mold to fit into us whatever we are lacking. It may be love, forgiveness, humility, or joy—whatever it is in your life that you need to be made complete in Him. If you have been feeling broken and disconnected lately, let God fill in your missing parts with His love and joy.

Swags

One of the most popular drapery designs requested in our business was the swag valance. Used with draperies or alone, the swag gave a real elegance to a room.

Sometimes we made swags that attached to a board, and we called that a more structured swag. We attached the fabric to the board with Velcro so the swag could be taken down and cleaned without taking the whole board down. Then, there are free-form swags. These swags are created by draping the fabric over a rod or through some holders. While there is less sewing on this type, it takes a lot more skill when it comes to creating the swag on the rod. I use double-sided carpet tape to hold the fabric on the rod and keep it in place.

Whatever design you decide on, you have to start with a bolt of fabric. That fabric doesn't look like much rolled up on the cardboard roller, but it has great potential. When it is unrolled and taken off the cutting table, it can be transformed into a beautiful design.

Just listen to Romans 12:12: "Don't copy the behavior and customs of this world, but let God transform you into a new person by changing the way you think. Then you will know what God wants you to do, and you will know how good and pleasing and perfect his will really is." What if that fabric said, "No, please don't take me off this roll. I am comfortable here all rolled up. Don't roll me out on that table where I will be inspected for flaws. And I certainly don't want anybody cutting me or sticking me with a needle and thread."

God wants to transform us, and that starts with our willingness to be transformed. He wants to renew our mind so we think differently. And if we think differently, then we will act differently. So give yourself over to the Master's hand today so He can transform you into a beautiful design.

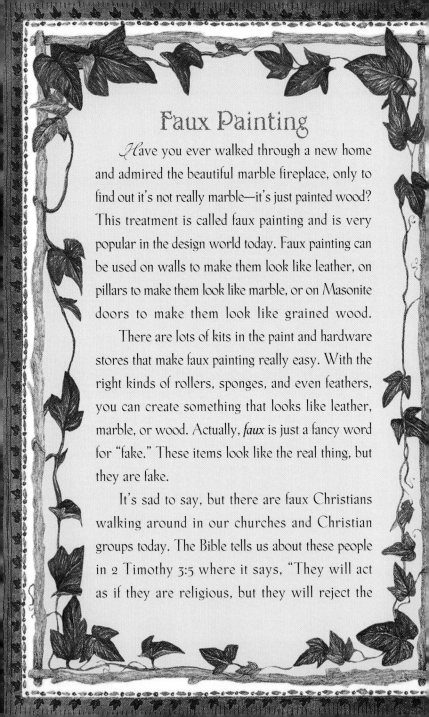

Faux Painting

*H*ave you ever walked through a new home and admired the beautiful marble fireplace, only to find out it's not really marble—it's just painted wood? This treatment is called faux painting and is very popular in the design world today. Faux painting can be used on walls to make them look like leather, on pillars to make them look like marble, or on Masonite doors to make them look like grained wood.

There are lots of kits in the paint and hardware stores that make faux painting really easy. With the right kinds of rollers, sponges, and even feathers, you can create something that looks like leather, marble, or wood. Actually, *faux* is just a fancy word for "fake." These items look like the real thing, but they are fake.

It's sad to say, but there are faux Christians walking around in our churches and Christian groups today. The Bible tells us about these people in 2 Timothy 3:5 where it says, "They will act as if they are religious, but they will reject the

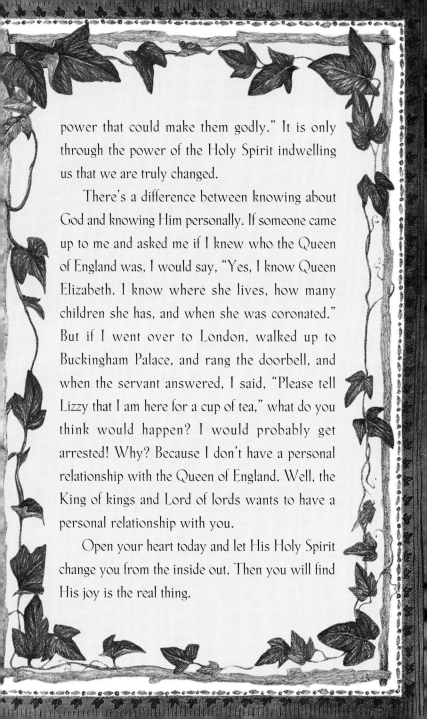

power that could make them godly." It is only through the power of the Holy Spirit indwelling us that we are truly changed.

There's a difference between knowing about God and knowing Him personally. If someone came up to me and asked me if I knew who the Queen of England was, I would say, "Yes, I know Queen Elizabeth. I know where she lives, how many children she has, and when she was coronated." But if I went over to London, walked up to Buckingham Palace, and rang the doorbell, and when the servant answered, I said, "Please tell Lizzy that I am here for a cup of tea," what do you think would happen? I would probably get arrested! Why? Because I don't have a personal relationship with the Queen of England. Well, the King of kings and Lord of lords wants to have a personal relationship with you.

Open your heart today and let His Holy Spirit change you from the inside out. Then you will find His joy is the real thing.

Planning

Many times I had clients come into my interior-design studio and want some help in decorating a new home. Most of the people couldn't afford to get everything at once, so I would help them work out a plan that would prioritize the items they could get right away and know what pieces would work when they could afford them. If you work up a floor plan and put the furniture templates in for the furniture you have and what you hope to get eventually, then you save yourself a lot of headaches later on.

You're not as tempted to buy an item on impulse and just hope it works in your plan. If you save for the pieces you want, it benefits you in two ways. One, it gives you time to pick just the right piece that will work in your room, and two, you're not paying interest on a purchase you just couldn't resist because it was such a good deal. After you figure all the interest charges on your purchase, you'll find out it wasn't such a bargain after all!

Remember Esau? He was so hungry when he came home that he couldn't wait to make something to eat, so he traded his birthright for a bowl of stew his brother had. Aren't we all like that sometimes? I call that the "Esau seesaw." The instant gratification of getting what we want gives us a high when we get it, but then sooner or later we come down hard on the pay dirt— whether it's a material possession we can't wait for, so we charge it, or sex before marriage because we couldn't wait for God's perfect timing.

Whatever it is in your life that's put you on that Esau seesaw, get off that track to nowhere and let God give you the fruit of self-control. You'll find there's a lot more joy in keeping your focus on God and letting Him give you His perfect gifts at just the right time.

Fellowship Friendly

I'm sure you've heard the phrase "user friendly." Today I am going to give you a few tips on how to make your home more fellowship friendly. By this I mean looking at ways to be prepared when you have guests over. It doesn't have to be a big group. Even just having a friend over for tea on the front porch can be fellowship.

I have a small round table on the front porch with two chairs for a quiet lunch or afternoon tea with a friend. You can have folding tables ready if you have more people over. With a tablecloth and centerpiece on them, they can look as festive as the regular furniture. The main thing to remember is to create an atmosphere where your friends can be comfortable and fellowship together.

This fellowship is an important part of our Christian lives. In 1 John 1:7 it tells us, "But if we are living in the light of God's presence, just as Christ is, then we have fellowship with each other, and the blood of Jesus, his Son, cleanses us from every sin." Our fellowship with other believers should go beyond just seeing them at church. We should get involved in each other's lives so we can pray for each other and build each other up in this common faith we have in Christ. Start a small group Bible study in your home, or have some friends over just to fellowship. Every few months I have a group of friends over for lunch at my house. We share our struggles and prayer concerns with each other and take time at the end to pray for each other. They have asked me for a schedule of my speaking engagements, so they can pray for me as I travel.

What a joy it is to know I have faithful friends praying for me each day. If you step out and take the initiative today, you will find abundant joy as you fellowship and share with other believers.

Balloon Shades

*H*ave you ever gone into a showroom or decorating display and admired the softly gathered balloon shade or balloon valance at the window? The balloon has a gathered or pleated top and then falls into poufs at the bottom, creating a soft, relaxed line. You need to use fabrics that have some body like chintz or polished cotton so the pouf at the bottom will stand out. If the fabric is too sheer or limp, it will droop and ruin the effect.

Balloon shades have cords that lift the shade to different heights and are usually attached to a board. If you are a do-it-yourselfer, you can find a pattern or instructions at a fabric store, but these are usually done professionally because they are so complicated. Whether you have a balloon valance or a balloon shade, the important thing is to get it to pouf out properly. Some people stuff tissues in the pouf, but I find a stiffer tissue paper works best, or those plastic grocery bags, but the main thing is to make sure the shade is puffed up.

Puffed up? Isn't there something in the Bible about being puffed up? No, it's not talking about balloon valances, rather about people who are puffed up! First Corinthians 4:7 (TLB) says, "What are you so puffed up about? What do you have that God hasn't given you? And if all you have is from God, why act as though you are so great, and as though you have accomplished something on your own?"

Many times we get so full of our own ambitions, plans, and pride that we get all puffed up and full of ourselves. God wants us empty and cleaned out so He can fill us with His Spirit. Come before God today and take out those tissues of disobedience, unforgiveness, pride, or whatever it is that has you puffed up, and let God fill you with His presence. He will fill you to overflowing with His love and joy!

Reminders

I was in a Christian bookstore recently and was amazed at the variety of Christian plaques, artwork, and decorative accessories that are available today. In choosing accessories for my husband's office, I found a beautiful picture of eagles in flight with a verse in Isaiah inscribed below it.

Some of the accessories we use in our homes can be reminders of God's love and faithfulness to us. When I get a pretty card with a verse on it, sometimes I put it in the window over my sink. I look at that card when I'm doing dishes, and it helps me memorize the verse while reminding me of the friend or loved one who sent it.

In our front foyer, we have a mahogany lowboy. In the center of that chest, on top of a round lace doily, I have an open Bible. At different times, someone in the family will open that Bible to a verse that has meant something special to him or her. It's almost like giving messages to each other with a secret codebook: God's codebook! Also, that open Bible right by the front door is a testimony to anyone coming into our home.

Another way to remind us of God's Word is by writing it on the wall—literally! A friend in Tennessee has the fruit of the Spirit list beautifully painted amid vines and flowers all around her daughter's bedroom. There are several wallpaper books available with borders that have Bible verses on them.

In Deuteronomy 6:6,7,9 the Lord says, "And you must commit yourselves wholeheartedly to these commands I am giving you today. Repeat them again and again to your children. Talk about them when you are at home and when you are away on a journey, when you are lying down and when you are getting up again....Write them on the doorposts of your house and on your gates." Let's create an atmosphere in our homes that helps us and our children to be reminded of God's goodness and faithfulness.

Special Chairs

When I was a little girl, we had a big green chair in the living room that was Daddy's special chair. I don't know what it was about that chair, but if Daddy wasn't home, we all wanted to sit in it. The only problem was it was made of loopy nylon upholstery, and the buckles on our little-girl shoes always got caught in it. Thank goodness they don't make that loopy nylon material anymore, and if you go into a furniture store today looking for a new chair, you will be amazed at all the styles, sizes, and colors available.

If you are trying to create a conversation area in a room, you may want to get two chairs alike to use on either side of the fireplace or to flank a table in front of a window. It's better to use chairs of different heights in the room so you have some variety. The taller chairs should be farther away from the entrance to the room, while a shorter chair can be closer to the doorway so you can see over it when you enter. For instance, if you have two high-back wing chairs on either side of the fireplace, then you may want to put a smaller club chair and ottoman at an angle facing the wing chairs. In a bedroom, a small chair is a convenient place for putting on your shoes or for curling up with a good book.

I remember sitting on Daddy's lap in that big green chair and having him read me a story. When I think back about sitting in that chair with my Dad, it reminds me of how we are seated in the heavenlies with Christ. Ephesians 2:6 tells us, "For he raised us from the dead along with Christ, and we are seated with him in the heavenly realms—all because we are one with Christ Jesus." Just as I had the right to climb up on my dad's lap because I was born into his family, we are seated with Christ in the heavenly realms because we are born into God's family. So if things start getting you down today, remember your position in Christ and let Him lift you up.

Ordinary

Sometimes we can take ordinary things we may have around the house and use them to create beautiful designs. Take PVC pipe, for instance. If you cover a piece of PVC pipe with fabric, it makes a wonderful rod on which to hang drapes or swags. If you have a bay window with little or no window casing for attaching rods, you can use cup hooks. Screw them on the casing above the window, pointing down, and a small brass rod can hang secured in the curve of the cup hook.

Use your imagination and you will begin to see the possibilities for using the ordinary to accomplish the extraordinary. We see God doing this very thing all through Scripture. He used ordinary people who were willing to be obedient to accomplish extraordinary things for Him.

Just think about Moses, an exiled shepherd and runaway, who was used to lead his people out of slavery. Or how about Mary, a simple peasant girl, who became the mother of Christ? And then there was Peter, an impulsive fisherman, who denied Christ three times when the pressure was on. But we see what happened when Peter stopped trying to do things on his own and let God's power surge through him. He became a bold witness, preaching to thousands, and wrote two books of the New Testament.

I think the late Rich Mullins said it best in one of his interviews when he stated that people who do great things for God don't set out to do great things for God. They are just obedient to the ordinary things God has called them to do, and then God makes great things happen. Come before God today empty of your own ambitions and let God fill you with His power. Then you will see how He can take the ordinary and make extraordinary things happen.

Toys

$\mathcal{D}$o you remember Christmas morning as a child and the excitement of finding a new doll or truck sitting under the tree? Many years have passed for some of us since those days, but there's no reason to keep those toys in a box in the attic.

Today I'm going to tell you how you can decorate with those old toys and revive memories of bygone days. My mother-in-law had a spare bedroom decorated just for our son, Brett, when he would visit, with some of my husband's old trucks and fire engines in it. We all took great pleasure in watching Brett play on the floor with those toys, just like his father had many years before. I have a little wicker carriage in my family room with my old doll, Mary, that I got for Christmas when I was five. I also have some old coloring books and a rag doll my grandmother made that's wearing a dress from an old feed sack. It's fun to reminisce about the times when I used to play with those toys as a child, but now I am grown, and I don't sit around and play with those toys like I used to.

Paul says something about this in 1 Corinthians 13:11: "When I was a child, I spoke and thought and reasoned as a child does. But when I grew up, I put away childish things." It's sad to see an adult who still has the mind of a child sitting around playing with toys all day. In the same way, it's sad to see Christians who have known the Lord for many years, but have never grown past the infancy stage in their Christian life. They sit in church every Sunday and want to be spoon-fed the Word, without ever feeding themselves during the week.

If you feel God speaking to your heart today about this, then start taking some steps to develop a more mature Christian walk. Get into His Word more. Join a Bible study. Be bolder in your witness for Christ. These are the things that will help you grow and experience the fulfillment of a joyful maturity in Christ.

Antiques

$\mathcal{D}$iscovering the beauty and mystery of old things is sometimes like going on a treasure hunt. You never know exactly what you're going to find as you dig through piles of musty, rusty, or dusty artifacts at shops, flea markets, or even yard sales. But once you've found a treasure at the bottom of an old box or in a dilapidated trunk, and you take it home, clean it up, and find out it's worth a lot more than you paid for it, then you're hooked!

Antiques can give your home a charm and individuality that can only be found in the beauty of old designs. Sometimes the expense of the original museum-quality antiques is beyond our reach, so we look at reproductions. There are many good, quality reproductions being manufactured today that look almost exactly like the original piece. Sometimes these beautiful, tasteful designs become favorite family heirlooms and are handed down through the family just like the originals were generations ago.

In the same way those reproductions are imitators of the original antiques, we should be imitators of Christ. Paul reminds us in Ephesians 5:1 (NIV) to "be imitators of God, therefore, as dearly loved children and live a life of love, just as Christ loved us and gave Himself up for us as a fragrant offering and sacrifice to God." If we want to look like Christ, we need to know Him intimately, and we can only do that by spending time with Him. Our relationship with Him will grow every day as we look into His Word and communicate with Him. As we grow closer and closer to Him, we will start to look more and more like Him. Eventually people will be drawn to the Jesus they see reproduced in *you*!

45

Skylights

I saw an ad in the home section of our Sunday paper. The sunshine was flooding the two-story foyer of this beautiful house, beaming down through the skylights. The caption read, "Our light comes from a higher source." Skylights are a great source of light and interest in kitchens, family rooms, bathrooms, and, of course, sunrooms. Skylights give 40 percent more light to a room than if you used the same size window in the wall. Skylights are not just great sources of light during the day, but on a clear, starry night they can be a dazzling window to heaven.

One evening after I finished the dishes, I went out into my darkened sunroom, sat in my rocker, and just gazed at the glorious, starlit sky. There were so many stars that I felt as if I could reach right up through the skylight and touch them. As I sat there, I thought of the time God said to Abram (whom He renamed Abraham), "Look up into the heavens and count the stars if you can. Your descendants will be like that—too many to count." Now, Abraham was a very old man, and humanly speaking, this seemed impossible. But the next verse, in Genesis 15:6, says "And Abram believed the LORD, and the LORD declared him righteous because of his faith."

So many times we are afraid to step out in faith because it looks like an impossible situation. But remember, nothing is too hard for the Lord! If we would just realize how powerful our God really is, we would see more of His power working in our lives. Our actions are outward demonstrations of what we believe in our hearts; that is, how much faith and confidence we have in God. Is there a situation in your life that looks impossible from a human point of view? Then step back and let God handle it—there's nothing too hard for our God!

Embroidery

Have you ever found a piece of embroidery and wondered what to do with it? Today I'm going to give you a few ideas on different ways to use embroidery in decorating.

If you have a pretty cross-stitched piece or embroidered picture, selecting the right frame is very important. I always use nonglare glass when framing embroidery so the glass will protect it, and glare won't detract from the beauty of the piece. A beautiful old hankie from your grandmother can be the back-drop of a shadowbox frame, grouped together with some other precious mementos from the family.

When my daughter, Heather, was little, I loved dressing her in little dresses that had embroidery or appliques. I took the smocked, embroidered bodice of one of her Polly Flinders' dresses when she outgrew it and made a throw pillow for her bed. She's 25 years old now and has a home of her own, but every time I make up that bed and see the pillow, it reminds me of how she looked in her little dress when she was three. I have one cross-stitched piece that I worked on when I was expecting my first baby. It looked okay from the front, but the back looked like a disaster with colorful threads crisscrossing each other.

That embroidered picture reminds me of a verse in Mark 8:33 where Jesus says, "You are seeing things merely from a human point of view, not from God's." So many times we look at the circumstances all around us, and it looks like the backside of that embroidered piece, all tangled and messy. If we would trust God and have faith that He's in control and creating something beautiful, we would have a lot more peace and joy.

The next time you get all tangled up by focusing on the troubles in your life, remember that the Master Designer is still working on you. Be still and let Him create the masterpiece He can see from His point of view.

Heirlooms

I have several heirlooms around my house that I have inherited from my grandparents or different relatives. Even if your home has a more contemporary look, you can use old things to accent and compliment the new.

For many years I had the old treadle Singer sewing machine cabinet from my grandmother in my sunroom. With the cabinet closed, it made a beautiful table for a bowl of colorful flowers. I've since given that old Singer to my daughter, Heather, who uses it in her guest room. The old Civil War rifle that was handed down to my father was then given by him to our son, Brett. The stories that go with those heirlooms are also handed down through the family. My husband, Doug, had some very old calendars that were given to him by his great-aunt. When we moved, we forgot and left them packed in a box in our new garage. We came upon that box after months had passed, and those calendars were all moldy and ruined. There are some things that we have kept for our children that will become their inheritance when we are gone. Now I'm very careful to keep those precious heirlooms in a safe place to preserve them.

As Christians we have an inheritance waiting for us. First Peter 1:4 tells us, "For God has reserved a priceless inheritance for his children. It is kept in heaven for you, pure and undefiled, beyond the reach of change and decay." Our inheritance of a place in heaven with God is securely waiting for us. We don't need to worry about it getting moldy or destroyed because God Himself is preserving it.

Let us look forward to that joyful day when we will finally receive the inheritance of all that God has prepared for us.

Measurements

I was never very good at math. It was one of my hardest subjects in school, and I thought it wasn't very important and I would probably never use it. Boy, was I wrong! I found out in college how important math and measurements are when working on a room design. Not only did I have to have the measurements of windows exact for window treatments and drapery rods, but also I had to figure square footage for wallpaper and carpeting.

The first week I worked as a designer in Washington, D.C., I had a call from a lady who had a yacht on the Potomac. She wanted window coverings for all the portholes on her yacht! I really had to dig down and try to remember my geometry, with all those radius and diameter measurements on the portholes! With circle windows, arched-top windows, and trapezoids, it's really a challenge figuring the dimensions!

There have been many times in my life when I have felt inadequate for the task I've had in front of me. I'm just so glad God takes measurements differently than we do. Remember Moses? Listen to what went on in Exodus 4:10,11: "But Moses pleaded with the LORD, 'Oh Lord, I am just not a good speaker. I never have been, and I'm not now, even after you have spoken to me. I'm clumsy with words.' 'Who makes mouths?' the Lord asked him. 'Who makes people so they can speak or not speak....Is it not I, the Lord?' " Sometimes we get nervous if we have to step out of our comfort zone and do something we're not used to or familiar with, but God never gives us something to do without giving us the power to do it. So the next time you feel as if you don't measure up, just step out and trust God. He's the one holding the measuring tape, and He's not measuring our ability, but our obedience.

Guests

I spend a lot of time traveling as I speak, and I've been invited to stay in a lot of different homes along the way. I love having people stay at our house, and now that our children are grown, we are free to offer our home whenever a speaker, preacher, missionary, or anyone comes through our town and needs a place to stay.

When you think about the guest room in your house, make sure it says, "welcome." Try to anticipate your guests' needs, and show them how much you care by the attention you have given to little details. It's always nice to have a place to put their suitcase. I have a chest at the end of the bed with a quilt over it. A rocking chair or a chair to relax in is always appreciated when your weary traveler wants to unwind and read. Make sure there's enough light to read by, and an alarm clock on the bedside table. One home I stayed in had a basket in the guestroom with samples of shampoo, mouthwash, a shower cap, and mints. I thought that was a good idea, and so I made a little welcome basket for my guest room and added lotion and a little sewing kit with safety pins. I try to put fresh flowers in the room before my guests come just to show them how special they are. Take a look around the room before your guests arrive and see if there's any way you can make it more comfortable.

It's a joy and privilege to share what God has given us with others, whether they are friends or strangers. First Peter 4:9 admonishes us to "cheerfully share your home with those who need a meal or a place to stay." So the next time there is a sign-up sheet for overnight hospitality for a visiting missionary or choir group, hurry and sign up. You'll find that when you reach out and share with others, you are the one who is blessed a hundred times over!

Garden Windows

The biggest problem I faced when remodeling kitchens was that they didn't have enough light. One of my favorite answers to that challenge was to put a bay window in the eating nook or a garden window over the sink. Actually, both of these solutions work, but the garden window lets the light shine in from above as well as from the front of the window. It's just great for growing little plants or herbs in the sill, and because the moisture from the sink is always floating upward, they really flourish.

If you don't have a room directly above your kitchen, a skylight is a great source of light. We have a skylight in our master bath, and it's so bright in there that my husband is always trying to turn off the light switch when he leaves—but it's already off! Sometimes, getting more light in your rooms is as simple as pulling back the draperies or taking them down altogether and putting up sheer curtains or swags. As the saying goes, "Let the sunshine in."

Ecclesiastes 11:7 (NIV) says, "Light is sweet, and it pleases the eyes to see the sun." I have a skylight in my sunroom, and as I rock back and forth in my glider rocker, sometimes I sing to the Lord. The sunlight flooding down through that window just washes over me and fills me with joy. But even that wonderful sunlight beaming down can't compare with the glorious joy we receive when the sunshine of God's love and forgiveness floods our soul.

Have you ever invited Jesus Christ into your life? If you haven't, He's just a prayer away. Ask Him to come in, change your heart, forgive you, and give you newness of life. Turn from your own way and toward Him, and He will flood you with the sunshine of His love and forgiveness.

51

Clocks

I remember sitting around the campfire singing a song about my grandfather's clock. Well, it's been a long time since I've sung that song, but I'll never forget the story about the old man and his beloved clock.

Clocks or timepieces are important elements of any good design. Not only are they necessary for telling us what time it is, but clocks used as an accessory or as a central furniture piece can be useful in designing a room.

I worked with one client who collected antique grandfather clocks. While one or two can enhance a room, sometimes too much of a good thing can be a problem when you're trying to achieve a tasteful, well-balanced design. If you have family heirloom clocks, you can group them together on a wall or in a special display cabinet. Of course, if they chime or ding, you could get pretty annoyed if they go off at the same time every hour!

Time is a funny thing. If you're doing something you don't like, time seems to drag on forever (ask any school child who watches the clock at the front of the classroom). Or as the saying goes, "time flies when you're having fun." But whatever you're doing, the 24 hours in every day are the same for everyone.

What are you doing with the time you've been given? Psalm 90:12 says, "Teach us to make the most of our time, so that we may grow in wisdom." Many days we get up in the morning, rush around, and go through the day in a blur without setting aside some quiet moments to spend with God. Time in His presence is time well spent, because He can teach us to make the most of it, and He gives us wisdom for whatever we come up against during the day.

The next time you look at the face of a clock, ask yourself if you've taken the time to look into the face of your Savior today. He's waiting patiently and wants to spend time with you.

Potential

Have you ever looked at a house that needs lots of work and been able to see the potential in that house? Sometimes we see these fixer uppers listed in the real estate magazines as "handyman specials." If you are willing to put a little elbow grease into a project like this, then you can come away with a real bargain. The key is to be able to see the potential in something that looks like a total disaster on the outside.

I usually suggest getting a reliable builder to look over the basic structure of the property to make sure the foundation, floor, and roof are all sound and in good condition. If you want to add on to the house, you should see an architect to design a room or rooms that will complement the overall atmosphere of the home. When your project is done, it gives you a great deal of satisfaction to see a beautiful home standing on the spot where there used to be a worn-out, old building...all because you could see what could be.

That's just how Jesus looks at us. He can see our potential, what we can become. In 1 John 3:2, we read, "Yes, dear friends, we are already God's children, and we can't even imagine what we will be like when Christ returns. But we do know that when he comes we will be like him, for we will see him as he really is." You see, before we accept Christ as our Savior, we look a lot like that dilapidated house, all dirty and worn and broken-down. But God can see the potential in us. After Christ enters our hearts, He starts rebuilding our lives. Sometimes it hurts when He tears down the walls and rips up the old flooring that we once stood on, but He is changing us to become more like Him.

If you feel as though your life is falling down around you, then let God change you from the inside out. He can see the potential in you, and you will become a beautiful home for Him as He resides in your heart.

Recliners

*D*o you remember your Dad's old recliner sitting in the corner of the living room? For many years recliners, as they are commonly known, have been the albatross or eyesore that decorators everywhere had to work around. But over the past few years, recliners have moved up in the fashion industry. Many of them have broken through the stereotype of Dad's old chair and become a central factor in designing a room because they are comfortable as well as beautiful.

There are recliners that look like Queen Anne chairs, as the footrest disappears under the chair when it is in an upright position. The chaise recliner has more padding, and the footrest connects with the seat so it supports the whole leg instead of just the feet. Also, recliners now come in different fabrics and leathers instead of just the corduroy or velours of the past.

When I see my husband, Doug, stretched out on his recliner after a hard day at work, I'm reminded of the verse in Hebrews 4:10 that says, "For all who enter into God's rest will find rest from their labors, just as God rested after creating the world." I've seen many people rushing around all the time, carrying burdens that they don't need to carry. They are carrying those burdens around like they are their cross to bear, and they want everybody to know how miserable they are.

If you recognize yourself here, then I encourage you to lay those burdens at God's feet and let Him carry them. The next time you kick back and relax in your recliner, just close your eyes and remember that God is able to carry all your burdens as you rest in the palm of His hand.

Mirrors

Mirror, mirror on the wall, who's the fairest of them all? While we may not always like what we see when we look in a mirror, it only reflects what is in front of it. In decorating we find that mirrors are a great way to enlarge rooms and reflect light. If you have a small room or entryway, you can visually double its size by mirroring one wall.

My dad is a dentist and wanted more light and interest in his windowless waiting room. We decided to make a window using a mirror, some window moldings, and a curtain. It gave the whole room a lighter, brighter feeling, and it was a real conversation piece.

In Colonial days, candles were the primary source of interior light. In order to get double the brightness from that candle, mirrors were placed behind the candles to reflect the light.

In 2 Corinthians 3:16–18 we read, "But whenever anyone turns to the Lord, then the veil is taken away....And all of us have had that veil removed so that we can be mirrors that brightly reflect the glory of the Lord. And as the Spirit of the Lord works within us, we become more and more like him and reflect his glory even more." Isn't that exciting? As we let God's Spirit work in us, we start to look more and more like Him. If we are clouded over by our own agendas, ambitions, and plans, then He can't shine through us. Let God have His way with you today so other people can see the reflection of your heavenly Father and His glory mirrored in you.

Swatches

In my interior-design business, we used a lot of fabric swatches, or samples. These little pieces of fabric were representatives of the real thing. Sometimes it's hard to visualize what a whole sofa is going to look like in a fabric you're only seeing a little piece of. That's why I had my upholsterer take the bolt of fabric to the client's house when he picked up a piece of furniture, so the client could see the effect when the fabric was rolled out. When we were doing draperies or bedspreads, we could usually get a yard of fabric to hold up to the window or over the bed so the client could get an idea of what it would look like. Those little pieces of fabric were necessary to get a picture of what the whole thing was going to look like when we were finished, but they could only give a small idea of the real thing.

As Christians we are supposed to be samples of what God is really like. Paul said in Ephesians 4:1,2, "Therefore I...beg you to lead a life worthy of your calling, for you have been called by God. Be humble and gentle. Be patient with each other, making allowance for each other's faults because of your love."

If someone looked at your life, could that person get an idea of what God is like? We all know that God is love, but are we showing others that we are a sample of that love by the way we live? You see a lot of those little bracelets with WWJD, which means "What Would Jesus Do?" I challenge you to let other people know you are a Christian, not by a bracelet you wear, but by the sample of God's love and joy they see radiating from you.

Seasons

*I*t's exciting seeing the changing seasons, and I love welcoming in each one by decorating my home. For spring I get out all the bunnies, chicks, and pastel silk flowers to perk everything up after a cold, dark winter. Then in summer I hang a floral basket on my front door and plant flowers all around the yard. Fall, with its brightly colored leaves and berries, makes for great-looking decorations on the mantelpiece and fireplace hearth. Then, of course, there's Christmas, with the array of holiday decorations, the Christmas tree, and all the trimmings.

With all these decorations, my attic just kept getting overcrowded, so I came up with a solution. I designed an arrangement that changes with the seasons! I got a plain green plastic bowl and made an arrangement of different-looking greens, ivies, and leaves. Then I would just change the base and add a few flowers or adornments to fit the season. In the spring I would put in some crocuses, violets, and daisies and put the whole thing in a pretty basket. The summer arrangement would have some silk begonias and a pretty bow. In the fall I used some grapes, berries, and pheasant feathers and put it in a hammered-brass container. At Christmas I put the arrangement in a tall silver bowl and used red velvet roses that looked real, along with some silver beads and balls.

Just as that arrangement changed for the seasons, we have different seasons in our lives—from growing up through our childhood, to falling in love, getting married, raising our children, and then seeing them grow to have homes of their own. I have seen all theses seasons in my life, but one thing stays the same. Jesus is the same yesterday, today, and forever. He's been there through all the ups and downs, and He will never fail. Let Him take your hand today, and He will guide you over the hills and valleys of the seasons in your life.

Mailboxes

I love pretty mailboxes. I had one client come to my studio (which I had in my home), and she said she knew I would have an interesting house because of the unique design of my mailbox. I looked all over trying to find an interesting post, then I bought a big white metal mailbox and had it painted with garlands and hummingbirds. There's a shop here in our little town that makes unique mailboxes that look like hobby horses, cows, or dogs. Whatever your fancy happens to be, you can find one to suit you. If you're adventurous, you can decorate your own mailbox with stencils, or let the children put a handprint on the mailbox with different colors and their names inscribed on the handprint so everyone will know who lives in your home.

But the best thing about mailboxes is opening them up and finding a letter or card from a friend or loved one. Did you ever realize that as Christians we are a letter from Christ? Just listen to what Paul says in 2 Corinthians 3:3: "Clearly, you are a letter from Christ prepared by us. It is written not with pen and ink, but with the Spirit of the living God. It is carved not on stone, but on human hearts." As God's children, we are His letter to the world. He has etched into our hearts by the Holy Spirit the message He wants the world to know.

What are you doing with the message of His love and forgiveness that He has imprinted on your heart? You might say, "I am not a good speaker" or, "I just don't know how to tell anyone about my faith." How about inviting a friend or neighbor to a Christian Women's Club or outreach dinner at your church? There are so many activities available to us, and we hear the message of Christ over and over, but what about those who have never heard it or understood it? Reach out to someone today, and let that person see the love and joy Christ has given you and the message He has etched on your heart.

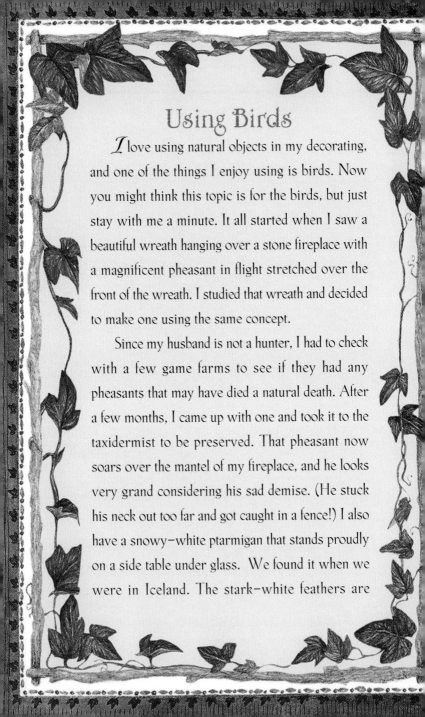

Using Birds

I love using natural objects in my decorating, and one of the things I enjoy using is birds. Now you might think this topic is for the birds, but just stay with me a minute. It all started when I saw a beautiful wreath hanging over a stone fireplace with a magnificent pheasant in flight stretched over the front of the wreath. I studied that wreath and decided to make one using the same concept.

Since my husband is not a hunter, I had to check with a few game farms to see if they had any pheasants that may have died a natural death. After a few months, I came up with one and took it to the taxidermist to be preserved. That pheasant now soars over the mantel of my fireplace, and he looks very grand considering his sad demise. (He stuck his neck out too far and got caught in a fence!) I also have a snowy-white ptarmigan that stands proudly on a side table under glass. We found it when we were in Iceland. The stark-white feathers are

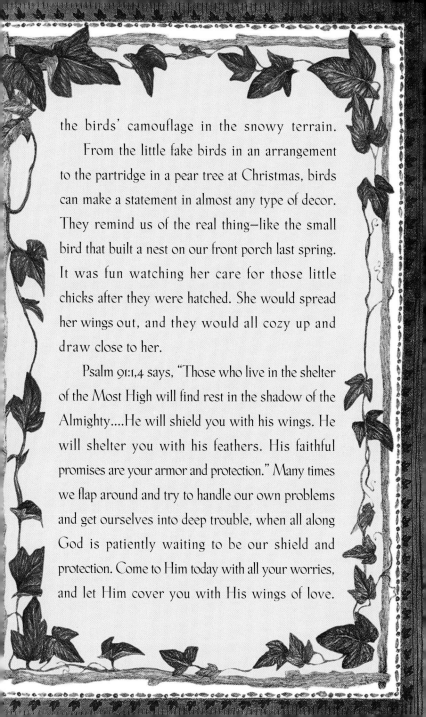

the birds' camouflage in the snowy terrain.

From the little fake birds in an arrangement to the partridge in a pear tree at Christmas, birds can make a statement in almost any type of decor. They remind us of the real thing—like the small bird that built a nest on our front porch last spring. It was fun watching her care for those little chicks after they were hatched. She would spread her wings out, and they would all cozy up and draw close to her.

Psalm 91:1,4 says, "Those who live in the shelter of the Most High will find rest in the shadow of the Almighty....He will shield you with his wings. He will shelter you with his feathers. His faithful promises are your armor and protection." Many times we flap around and try to handle our own problems and get ourselves into deep trouble, when all along God is patiently waiting to be our shield and protection. Come to Him today with all your worries, and let Him cover you with His wings of love.

Balance

As I worked with clients on room plans, there were many things to take into consideration: colors, scale, style, and of course, balance. Today we're going to look at balance, both symmetrical and asymmetrical.

Symmetrical balance means that there is the same thing on either side of an imaginary line. If your mantelpiece is symmetrical, then there are identical vases, candles, or whatever on each side of the mantel. If you are using asymmetrical design, then you have different items on each side, but they are balanced. Maybe there are two tall candles on one side and a cascading ivy plant on the other. They are different items, but they balance each other. The trick here is to make sure you don't have one side overpowering the other so your arrangement looks lopsided.

Sometimes we feel overpowered in our

lives and we get out of balance. It might be a rebellious teenager, tension in our marriage, or stress at work. Whatever happens in our lives, we need to keep our focus on God and trust Him to work things out. In 2 Corinthians 4:17 we read, "For our light and momentary troubles are achieving for us an eternal glory that far outweighs them all."

If you feel like there are too many things piling up on your side of the mantelpiece, just remember, God is at work keeping everything in balance on His side. Keep loving and trusting God, and someday you will look back and see clearly His purpose worked out for your good. Trust God to keep things balanced in your life, and you will get through each day with more assurance of His peace and joy.

Irritants

Have you ever looked around your house and thought to yourself, "If I could just get rid of that, I would be okay." Maybe it's the avocado shag rug in the living room or the harvest–gold refrigerator in the kitchen, or the orange vinyl in the foyer. Whatever it is, it's an eyesore that you would love to eliminate! So many times we have to work around things that are real irritants. The best thing to do is just ignore the problem and decorate around it until you have the money to replace it. Accentuate the positive and play down the negative.

I find that's what I have to do with people who irritate me, too. I try to handle my irritations differently now than I used to. If someone cuts me off on the road, I try to smile and wave and think, "That poor man must have a lot of stress to be in such a hurry." Or if I encounter a grouchy salesclerk, I smile and think, "That poor woman must be having a bad day." Now don't get me wrong, I get flustered just like everyone else. It's almost a game I play and a challenge to see if I can get through an irritation without losing my cool.

That verse in Romans 12:18 reminds us to "do your part to live in peace with everyone, as much as possible." If there are irritants in your life that you have to work around, ask God to help you see those people through His eyes. You might be the only Jesus they ever see, so make sure you're a good representative of Him. The next time you encounter irritating people or circumstances, remember the voice that comes over the radio and says, "This is a test." If you come through that test with flying colors, it will please the Lord and give you abundant satisfaction and joy.

Lamp Shades

When you see a beautiful lamp, a large part of the overall design of that lamp is the lamp shade. If the lamp shade is too big for the lamp, then the lamp looks dumpy. If the shade is too small, then you can see the bulb and it looks funny. So, choosing the right shade for your lamp is very important.

Not only is size important when choosing a shade, but you also need to consider shape, color, fabric, and sometimes even pattern. You can add interest and color in accenting your room with a shade that is floral or has some design on it.

My sister, Becky, took a pierced lamp shade class. Cutting and piercing the paper of the shade created a beautiful design when the light filtered through the pierced and cut openings of the shade.

When I saw that shade, it reminded me of what happens sometimes to Christians who don't let their light fully shine for the Lord. Matthew 5:15,16 says, "Don't hide your light under a basket! Instead, put it on a stand and let it shine for all. In the same way, let your good deeds shine out for all to see, so that everyone will praise your heavenly Father." When we are in a right relationship with God, then His light shines in us. Sometimes we let sin, unforgiveness, or bad attitudes dim our lights, and we can't shine for Jesus like we should. Is there something in your life that has shaded your testimony for the Lord? Confess that sin today, and let God help you be all He had in mind when He made you. When His light shines through you, then you can reach out to other people and they will see the radiance of God's presence in you.

Canopy

When my daughter, Heather, was a little girl, I decided to let her help me decorate her room. She wasn't too concerned about the color or the furniture. The thing she wanted most was a canopy bed. We couldn't afford to buy her a canopy bed, so I made her a canopy. I placed her twin size bed under the window in her room and put sheers over the window. I had my husband cut a semicircle out of a piece of plywood and place it over the top of the window with angle irons projecting out from the wall. I then took a lightweight peach fabric and attached it to the covered plywood piece, draping and swagging the fabric down around the head of her bed. When it was finished, she said she felt like a princess. You can also make a frame the same size as the bed out of PVC pipe. If you shirr a filmy fabric onto all the rods and suspend them from the ceiling over the bed, you have created a beautiful canopy.

When you look at a canopy bed, there is a feeling of cozy protection and serenity. It reminds me of God's canopy of protection that continually hovers over us. David reminds us in Psalm 105:39 that "the LORD spread out a cloud above them as a covering and gave them a great fire to light the darkness." Just as the Lord took care of His people in the wilderness, He's continually watching over His children today.

There's nothing that happens in our lives that God doesn't know about. So if you are fearful or worried about your future, don't let it get you down. God is in control, and His canopy of protection is always over us.

Patterns

I learned how to use patterns in Mrs. Diehl's seventh-grade sewing class. All those pieces of transparent golden tissue paper looked like foreign objects to me as I pulled them out of the envelope and tried to arrange and pin them onto my fabric. Eventually I got the hang of it, and through the years I've realized how important it is to follow the pattern.

When I attended college, I was using patterns to tailor coats, make draperies, and cover furniture. After a while, I was making my own patterns for cornices, window treatments, and all kinds of designs. It was great seeing how the design sketched out on paper eventually became a reality that could actually be touched and seen. If you go into the sewing stores today, there are many patterns for throw pillows, window treatments, and all kinds of accessories. Actually, if you know how to follow a pattern, there's no limit to all the wonderful things you can make for your wardrobe or home.

All of us are following a pattern in our lives whether we realize it or not. In 2 Timothy 1:13 Paul admonishes Timothy to "hold on to the pattern of right teaching you learned from me. And remember to live in the faith and love that you have in Christ Jesus." We need to follow the pattern given to us in God's Word as we try to assemble our lives.

So many times we try to do things on our own and attempt to cut on the fabric of our lives without following the pattern. Also, we serve as a pattern to our children and younger Christians who look to us to see how it's done as we travel down this road of life. We need to keep ourselves so closely pinned to the faith and love we have in Jesus Christ that when others use us as their pattern, they will really be seeing God's design etched out on us.

Boxes

*D*on't you just love getting a gift in a pretty box? I have so many pretty boxes, that I started decorating with them. When I hosted a Victorian tea party, hatboxes decorated with pretty paper were centerpieces on the dining room table. Lace doilies, strings of pearls, old pictures, and pink roses were spilling out of each box, and everyone loved it. At Christmas I wrapped plain boxes in foil with pretty ribbon and used them on the front porch in a sleigh along with some toys and pine garlands. If you have a lot of those little velvet boxes, try putting some small silk or dried flowers in each one and using them as a gift at each place setting when you have a dinner party or luncheon with special friends.

It's fun seeing all the different ways you can use boxes. In a real sense we are boxes or containers for God's gift. In 2 Corinthians 4:7 it says, "But this precious treasure—this light and power that now shine within us—is held in perishable containers, that is, in our weak bodies. So everyone can see that our glorious power is from God and is not our own." You see, God could have chosen beautiful, perfect containers for the gift of His Spirit, but He used us in our weak frailty to be His temple.

It is only when we come to Him in absolute surrender and empty ourselves of our own plans and ambitions that we are empty enough for Him to fill with His power. Every time I go out to speak my prayer is that God will put His thoughts in my mind and His words in my mouth and let His Spirit be the power that works through me.

So the next time you look in the mirror, don't worry about that perishable container staring back at you. Just remember, you have been entrusted with the precious treasure of God's light and power, so let it *shine*!

Conversation Areas

Have you ever been sitting in a room at a party and trying to hold a conversation with someone seated too far away? Many times when we arrange our living room or family room, we place the furniture too far apart. What you want to do when you arrange your sofa and chairs in a room is create a pleasing conversation area. The rule of thumb is to place furniture no more than ten feet apart so your guests can talk easily and can hear each other.

If you have a large room, you may want to create two conversation areas. Think about placing your furniture in the center of the room if your room is large, or bringing in extra seating from the dining room when you have company. Whichever way you set up your conversation area, make sure the furniture is arranged so your guests can enjoy talking to each other without shouting across the room.

There's a verse in Ephesians 4:29 that tells us how to guard the conversation that comes out of our mouths. It says, "Don't use foul or abusive language. Let everything you say be good and helpful, so that your words will be an encouragement to those who hear them." I've heard it said that the most dangerous member of our bodies, the one that can do the most damage, is our tongue. If you gossip about someone or put him or her down in front of other people, the negative reflection is not on them, but on you. As Christians, we should be careful to lift each other up and keep our conversations wholesome and clean.

The next time you are tempted to "get the inside scoop" when you're with some of your friends, turn the conversation around to a topic that is more pleasing to God. If you do that, you will be showing forth more of His love and joy.

Lost Treasures

*I*t was a hot, sticky day in the middle of summer, and my daughter, Heather, was bored. School wouldn't start for another six weeks, and she and her friend wanted something to do. My sister Becky, was planning a yard sale at her home, so I suggested that the girls clean out our garage, basement, and Heather's closet and join the yard sale. Much to my surprise, they were excited about the idea (I am sure it was the lure of extra money and not the desire to clean the closet that was the clincher). Those girls came up with several boxes of stuff to sell at the yard sale. Heather and her friend left early the next morning to set up all their merchandise.

Later on in the morning, I drove over to my sister's house to see how things were going. As I browsed through the boxes and tables set up around the yard, my heart sank as I spotted a little toy truck. That little toy truck was from a collection of antique toys I had saved in a box that had been handed down from my husband's family through several generations. When I asked where the other toys were from that box, my daughter proudly informed me that an antique dealer had been the first one there in the morning and had bought almost the whole box! She joyfully waved the ten-dollar bill he had given her for the lot. As I bemoaned the loss of our precious heirlooms, I realize it was my mistake for not looking over Heather's "junk."

We all make mistakes in our lives, and the worst thing we can do is to keep dwelling on those mistakes. Paul tells us in Philippians 3:13, "No, dear friends, I am still not all I should be, but I am focusing all my energies on this one thing: Forgetting the past and looking forward to what lies ahead." The mistakes and sins of our past put blinders on us so we can't see the joy that lies ahead. So if you're living in that echoing cave of "if only" or "what if" then give it up and let Jesus lead you into the sunshine of His hope and joy.

A Closing Word

I would love to sit down with each one of you, have tea at your kitchen table, and share ideas on decorating your home. Unfortunately, I can't—so this little book is the next best thing. I had fun writing down these ideas and quick tips that can be done right away. I hope you have discovered some ideas on what you can do in your home to make it more beautiful and welcoming.

As I travel and speak, I meet women from all walks of life who want to create a beautiful and inviting atmosphere in their homes. Today, Designs for Living is touching many through radio, TV, and personal speaking engagements, using interior design as a bridge to reach people with the truth of God's Word.

If this book has helped bring more joy into your home and your life, we would love to hear from you. Write us at:

DESIGNS FOR LIVING
P.O. BOX 37
DANVILLE, PA 17821
Or check out our website at:
www.designsforliving.org